Garan Holcombe

Super Grammar

Practice Book Level 4

CAMBRIDGE
UNIVERSITY PRESS

Contents

Simple present questions

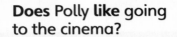

Does Polly **like** going to the cinema?

Yes, she does. She goes every week!

Super Grammar

Use **simple present** questions to ask people about habits and routines.

Yes/No questions are formed with *be* or *do*:

Are you from Izmir?	Yes, I am. No, I'm not.
Are we/they from Istanbul?	Yes, we/they are. No, we/they aren't.
Is he/she from Bursa?	Yes, he/she is. No, he/she isn't.
Do you/we/they like playing the guitar?	Yes, I/we/they do. No, I/we/they don't
Does he/she love watching films?	Yes, he/she does. No, he/she doesn't.

'Wh' questions are formed by putting *where, what, why,* etc., before *do*:

What is your favourite type of music?

1 Complete the questions with either *do/does* or the correct form of *be*.

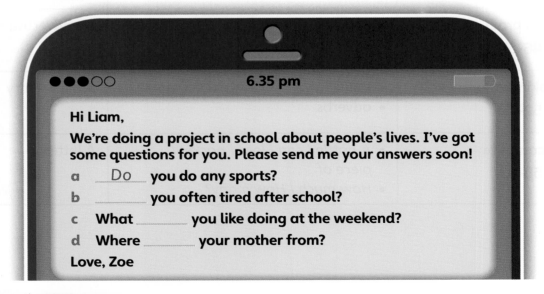

●●●○○   6.35 pm

Hi Liam,

We're doing a project in school about people's lives. I've got some questions for you. Please send me your answers soon!

a   __Do__   you do any sports?

b   _____ you often tired after school?

c   What _____ you like doing at the weekend?

d   Where _____ your mother from?

Love, Zoe

2 **Match the questions from Exercise 1 with the answers below.**

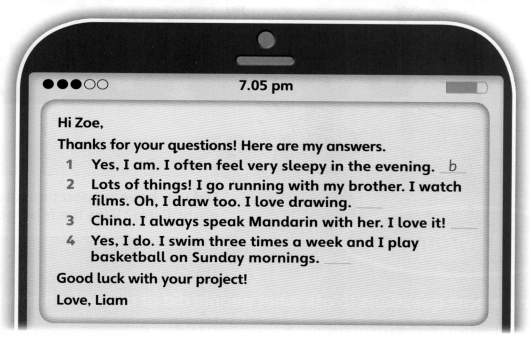

Hi Zoe,

Thanks for your questions! Here are my answers.

1   Yes, I am. I often feel very sleepy in the evening. _b_

2   Lots of things! I go running with my brother. I watch films. Oh, I draw too. I love drawing. ___

3   China. I always speak Mandarin with her. I love it! ___

4   Yes, I do. I swim three times a week and I play basketball on Sunday mornings. ___

Good luck with your project!

Love, Liam

3 **Complete the dialogue with the words from the box.**

> does   ~~what~~   don't   who   live   Yes

Mehmet: ¹ _What_ does your brother do, Nick?

Nick: He's a journalist.

Mehmet: Really! Is it an exciting job?

Nick: I ² _____ know. I think he likes it.

Mehmet: ³ _____ does he work for?

Nick: He writes for the *El País* newspaper. In Spain.

Mehmet: What ⁴ _____ he write about?

Nick: He interviews famous people. Actors, singers.

Mehmet: Does he ⁵ _____ in Madrid

Nick: ⁶ _____, he does. In a place called La Latina.

Simple past questions

> **Did** you **have** a good time at the party, Petra? **Was** the food good?

Super Grammar

Use **simple past questions** to ask what people did at a specific time in the past.

Yes/No questions are formed with *was/were* or *did*:

Were you at the park yesterday? Yes, I was.   No, I wasn't.
Was he/she in the cinema?   Yes, he/she was   No, he/she wasn't.

The question form with *did* is the same for every person, i.e. *I, he, she, they*:
Did you/he/she/we/they go surfing?

'Wh' questions are formed by putting *Where, What, Why*, etc., before *was/were* and *did*:
Where were you on Saturday?   Where did you go on holiday?

---

1 **Complete the questions and answers about Kitty's holiday in Italy.**

1   _Were_ you happy on holiday?   Yes, we _were_ .

2   _____ your brother with you?   No, he _____ . He had to work.

3   _____ you go to Venice?   No, we _____ . We went to Rome.

4   _____ your parents like Italy?   Yes, they _____ . They want to go back next year!

5   _____ the people friendly?   Yes, they _____ . They taught me some Italian.

2 Are the questions correct or incorrect? Correct the questions you think are wrong.

1 What do you do yesterday?
   incorrect   _What did you do yesterday?_

2 Were you at school yesterday?

3 Do you go to the beach last summer?

4 Was you tired this morning?

5 What was the last film you saw?

6 Do you did your homework last night?

3 Answer the questions from Exercise 3.

1

2

3

4

5

6

Reading: a poem

1 Read the poem, then order the six questions from it.

The Questioner

Do you like your school, your house, your life
Do you eat your food with a fork and knife?
Do you have adventures big and small,
Do you think of yesterday at all?
When you were young
What did you do?

Did you go on dodgems bright and new?
Were rollercoasters white and blue?
On roundabouts without a care
Did the boys and girls have golden hair?
Are you different now
You know much more?
Or are you as you were before?

The simple past is present now
The moments come and go and how
We go on asking questions, yes,
But what's the last one?
Can you guess?

a   When you were young what did you do? _____

b   Are you different now? _____

c   Were rollercoasters white and blue? _____

d   Do you like your school, your house, your life? __1__

e   What's the last one? _____

f   Do you have adventures big or small? _____

Writing

1 **Match the words with the definitions.**

1 rhythm
2 rhyme
3 verse
4 poet
5 poem

a this is writing with short sentences (called lines) and using words that often rhyme

b this is someone who writes poems

c when the end of two words have the same sound, e.g. *cat/hat*, *blue/do*, *door/floor*

d this is how the words sound together

e this is a group of lines that forms part of a poem; 'The Questioner' has three of these

Help with Writing

Poems are not easy to write in another language. Think of words that rhyme, e.g. *fat, hat, cat, mat*. Then try writing a simple poem with a simple rhythm, e.g. *My dog is fat, he wears a hat, he hates the cat, she chews his mat.*

2 **Complete the poem with the words from the box.**

> me   Jo   floors   low

The Treasure Hunt

'Where is the gold, the gold?' said Lee,
'What gold? What gold?' said Tom
to ¹ ___me___
I did not know, so turned to go,
And talk to Sue and Mark and
² _____ .

We looked at maps, for clues and doors
And holes in walls and wooden
³ _____ ,
We looked up high, we looked down ⁴ _____ ,
Until it was our time to go.

3 **Now write another verse for the poem. Follow the rhythm of the verses.**

1 Must / Mustn't

> You **mustn't take** photographs of the paintings and you **must turn** your mobile phones off.

Super Grammar

Use **must** to talk about what it is necessary to do, e.g. *I must buy my mother a birthday card.*
Use **mustn't** to tell someone not to do something, e.g. *You mustn't play the drums so loudly.*

We do not add an *–s* to the third person with *must*. We say *he must do his homework* not ~~he musts do his homework~~.

1 **Read what Maria says then circle the correct verbs to complete the sentences.**

'Mum and Dad say I don't do enough to help them with the chores. I'm going to show them how much I can do. To help me, I've got a list of things I must and mustn't do. I'm going to put it on my wall in my room …'

1 I *must* / *mustn't* tidy my room at least once a month.

2 I *must* / *mustn't* leave my clothes on the floor.

3 I *must* / *mustn't* wash the dishes at weekends.

4 I *must* / *mustn't* help Dad in the garden on Sunday afternoons.

5 I *must* / *mustn't* help Mum wash her car once a month.

6 I *must* / *mustn't* put dirty plates on the floor.

2 Complete the story with the verbs from the box.

> clean ~~wear~~ be learn toast use

The Never-ending Orders of Old King Marvin

Old King Marvin lived in a huge castle near Learnum Wood.
His favourite thing was telling people what to do. 'You ¹mustn't
___wear___ your crown in the garden,' he said every morning to
Good Queen Tess.'It might fall off.' A handsome young knight
called Gordon the Magnificent lived in the castle too. 'You must ² _____ your
shield and helmet,' Old King Marvin said to Gordon. 'And you must ³ _____
how to use your sword. But you mustn't ⁴ _____ it inside the castle.'

One morning Old King Marvin went to the kitchen. 'I would like to make breakfast
this morning,' he said to the cook. 'Is that all right?' 'Yes, sir.' said the cook. Ten
minutes later Good Queen Tess heard a loud voice in the kitchen. 'I'm very sorry,
sir, but you must ⁵ _____ the bread for thirty-three seconds longer. You must
⁶ _____ careful with bread. It's easy to get it wrong.' Good Queen Tess smiled
to herself, happy to hear someone telling her husband what to do for a change.

3 Look at the pictures. Write sentences with *must* and *mustn't*.

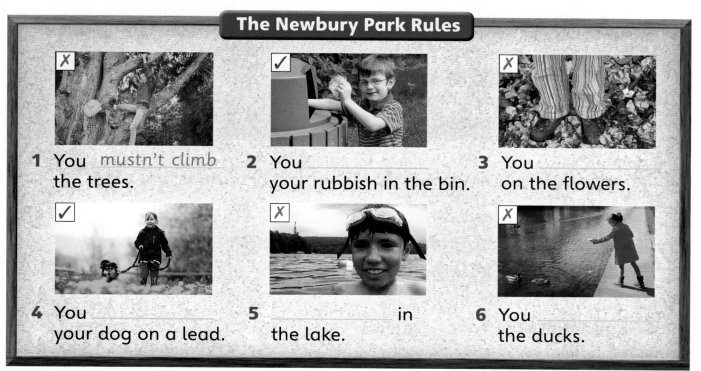

The Newbury Park Rules

1 You *mustn't climb* the trees.

2 You _____ your rubbish in the bin.

3 You _____ on the flowers.

4 You _____ your dog on a lead.

5 _____ in the lake.

6 You _____ the ducks.

Direct and indirect objects

> Juanita, give **him the ball**, please.

Super Grammar

Use **direct and indirect objects** to talk about things or people affected by the action of the verb.

Subject	Verb	Indirect object	Direct object
Jeremy	gave	David	the book.
I	made	my sister	a sandwich.
Don't	show	me	the answer.

The direct object is the person or thing affected by the action of the verb. It answers the question 'what', e.g. *What did Jeremy give to David?*

The indirect object is also the person or thing affected by the action of the verb; it answers the question 'who', e.g. *Who did Jeremy give the book to?*

We sometimes put the indirect object at the end of the sentence, where it usually follows the prepositions *to* and *for*.

Jeremy gave the book to David.   *Don't show the answer to me.*
I made a sandwich for my sister.

---

1 **Replace the underlined words with object pronouns.**

1 My brother and I gave a <u>necklace</u> to <u>Mel</u>.   <u>My brother and I gave it to her.</u>

2 She gave <u>the book</u> to <u>Stan and Toni</u>.   _____

3 They gave <u>the book</u> to <u>Tim</u>.   _____

4 He gave <u>the book</u> to <u>his mother</u>.   _____

5 She gave <u>the book</u> to <u>my father</u>.   _____

6 He gave <u>the book</u> to <u>my brother and me</u>.   _____

2 **Rewrite the sentences with the words in the correct order.**

1 Show the bracelet me, please.   _Show me the bracelet, please._

2 Don't the story tell Juan.   _____

3 You must buy the dress Gabriella.   _____

4 I gave the belt Wang Li to.   _____

5 I bought Sheila for a hat.   _____

6 Sarah give the necklace.   _____

3 **Complete the paragraph with the following pronouns: *it*, *her*, *them*, *us*, *me*.**

Mr. James and The Bag of Sweets

'Give ¹ _them_ to ² _____, please'
said Mr James.

'But the sweets are Sandra's, Mr James.'
said Sonny.

'Yes, I know the sweets are Sandra's,
but don't give ³ _____ back to ⁴
_____. It's not break time. You know
the rule.'

'Yes, Mr James I know ⁵ _____;
you remind ⁶ _____ all every day –
we mustn't eat sweets in class.'

'Anything,' said Mr James. 'You
mustn't eat anything in class. Come on,
then. Sandra can have ⁷ _____ back
at break time.'

I gave Mr James the bag of sweets
and sat in my chair. Five minutes later,
I looked up from my Maths book.

'Mr James!' I said. 'You're eating
⁸ _____. But you said …'

'Yes, I know I did, Sonny,' said Mr
James, smiling, 'but they really are
very nice sweets.'

Reading: a postcard

 Read the postcard then answer the questions.

Dear Eve,

Yesterday we went to the fantastic Chocolate Museum. You must go there!

A guide told us all about the history of chocolate and we watched a short film about how to make chocolate. Dad thought the film was great. They had a brilliant collection of old chocolate wrappers too – Grandma really liked that.

They also gave us some free chocolate to take home. It was delicious!

I hope you are well.

Love

Li Yan

Eve Blackburn

23, January Street

Belfast

Northern Ireland

BT9 5AB

1 Where did Li Yan and her family go?
They went to the Chocolate Museum.

2 What did the guide tell them about?

3 Who thought the film was very good?

4 Who liked the collection of old chocolate wrappers?

5 What did they get to take home?

Writing

1 Complete the descriptions of the museums with *must* or *mustn't*.

The Football Museum

You **1** _must_ come to the Football Museum! All fans of the beautiful game **2** _____ miss it. See the shirt Pele wore in the 1970 World Cup Final. Watch a film about how football began.

The SWORD MUSEUM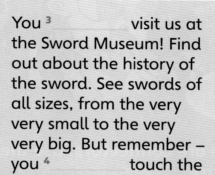

You **3** _____ visit us at the Sword Museum! Find out about the history of the sword. See swords of all sizes, from the very very small to the very very big. But remember – you **4** _____ touch the swords!

The Royal Museum

The Royal Museum tells the story of Europe's kings and queens. You **5** _____ ask your History teacher to bring you here. Learn all about the kings of Spain and Harald Fairhair, the first king of Norway.

Help with Writing

We usually write postcards to describe our experiences to friends and family. We often use adjectives such as *brilliant*, *great* and *fantastic* to talk about what we did.

2 Imagine you went to one of the museums in Exercise 1. Write a postcard to tell a friend about it. Use Li Yan's postcard to help you.

2 Connectors

We stayed in a lovely village **and** we went swimming every day. Lola didn't swim **because** the water was really cold!

Super Grammar

And, *but*, *so* and *because* are **connectors**. Use them to join two parts of a sentence.

Use *and* and *but* to connect two ideas. Use *but* when the second idea is different to the first. Use a comma before *but*.

We had picnics in the fields and we walked through the forest. I liked having picnics, but I didn't like walking through the forest

Use *because* and *so* to talk about the reasons for an action. Use a comma before *so*.

I was tired, so I went home. I went home because I was tired.

1 **Circle the correct connectors to complete the sentences.**

1 We went to the village _____ we climbed the mountain.

   a so   **b** (and)   **c** but

2 We walked by the river, _____ we didn't swim in it.

   a but   **b** because   **c** and

3 We wanted to go on the river, _____ we took a boat to the island.

   a but   **b** and   **c** so

4 We went back to the village early _____ Mum was sleepy.

   a because   **b** and   **c** so

2 **Complete the poem with *and*, *so*, *but* or *because*.**

The Park Poem

It was a beautiful day,
¹ _____So_____ we all went to play,
We laughed ² _____ we joked quite a lot,
We sat in the shade
Of a towering tree
³ _____ we were hungry and hot.
After sandwiches, chocolate,
Bananas and more,
We were sleepy, ⁴ _____ then Ricky said,
'I don't know about you,
My two favourite friends,
⁵ _____ I think I'm ready for bed.'

3 **Complete the sentences in the paragraph with your own ideas.**

My Weekend

On Friday, I did my homework ¹ _and had my dinner_ . I didn't go to the
cinema ²because _____ . On Saturday morning I was really hungry, so
³ _____ . On Saturday afternoon, I went to Dominic's birthday party,
but ⁴ _____ . On Sunday morning it was sunny, so ⁵ _____ .
I usually go to my grandparents' house on Sunday afternoons, but last
Sunday ⁶ _____ because _____ . On Sunday evening I watched
TV and ⁷ _____ . I went to bed early because ⁸ _____ .

Could/Couldn't

What **could** you **do** when you were young, Grandma?

Oh, I **could do** lots of things, my dear. I **could walk** for hours, but not get tired. I **could run**, I **could swim** and I **could go** ice skating. And these days, I can do jigsaw puzzles. There – that's the final piece!

Super Grammar

Use **could/couldn't** to talk about abilities you had or didn't have in the past,
When she was a girl she couldn't swim, but she could ride a bike.
Yes/no questions are formed in the following way:

Could you/he/she/we/they make pancakes?
Yes, I could/he/she/we/they could.
No, I/he/she/we/they couldn't.

1 **Answer the questions with *Yes, I could* or *No, I couldn't*.**

1 Could you walk when you were six months old?   No, I couldn't
2 Could you speak when you were one year old?   _____
3 Could you run when you were three years old?   _____
4 Could you catch a ball when you were four years old?   _____
5 Could you read when you were five years old?   _____
6 Could you write when you were seven years old?   _____

2 **Complete the questions with the verbs from the box.**

speak   play   climb   ~~run~~   ski   ride

www.theoldpeopleswebsite.co.uk

The Old People's Website

When you were a young man ...

1 Could you *run* fast?

2 Could you _____ mountains?

3 Could you _____ any other languages?

4 Could you _____ the guitar?

5 Could you _____ a motorbike?

6 Could you _____ or snowboard?

3 **Match the questions in Exercise 2 with the answers.**

a No, I couldn't, but my brother could. He was part of a club. He went up Everest once! __2__

b Yes, I could. I didn't like driving cars, but I loved bikes. I had a second-hand Harley Davidson! _____

c No, I couldn't. I didn't go on winter holidays. They were too expensive! _____

d No, I couldn't. I could play the violin, but I didn't learn to play anything else. _____

e Yes, I could. I lived in Buenos Aires for five years when I was in my twenties, so my Spanish was very good. _____

f Yes, I could. I loved doing that. I used to run by the river near my house every morning. _____

Reading: a story

1 **Read the story. Then complete the summary with the words from the box.**

The Strange Tale of Jim Garry's Mountain

It was the Mayor who saw it first. 'Another beautiful morning,' he said to himself as he opened his curtains. 'Wait a moment. Jim Garry's Mountain is …'

It was all the villagers could talk about. 'How can we climb it now?' they asked. Everyone was very worried, so they met in the Town Hall that evening to discuss the problem. 'Thank you all for coming ,' said the Mayor, 'Now as you know, Jim Garry's mountain is …'

'It's not just Jim Garry's Mountain,' said a voice.

An old man near the door stood up. His long hair and beard were grey.

'Excuse me,' said the Mayor, 'this meeting is for the people of the village only.'

'Don't you want to know what's happening? Why there is no water in the river and no grass in the fields?'

'What are you talking about? We are here to talk about where our mountain went.'

'Everything is going because you don't look after it.'

'You must care for the world around you, Mayor. That is all I want to say. Good evening to you.'

The villagers were more interested in who the man was than what he had to say. Nobody noticed that the forests, fields, lakes and islands were not there anymore. The only thing left in the village was the Town Hall and the people in it.

---

mountain   Town Hall   Mayor   people   village   rivers

One morning, the Mayor of the ¹ _village_ finds that the ² _____ is not there. The ³ _____ of the village are very worried. They have a meeting in the ⁴ _____ . At the meeting, an old man that nobody knows says why everything is going from the village – the trees, the ⁵ _____ , the lakes. The ⁶ _____ is not very happy with the old man. The old man leaves and the people talk about him. They do not notice what is happening around them.

Writing

1 **Match the story types with the definitions.**

1 comedy

2 history

3 fantasy

4 romance

5 science-fiction

a a story about something that happened in the past

b a story about things that aren't real or things that can't happen, e.g. in real life people can't fly

c a story that makes us laugh

d a story about technology, the future and space

e a story about people who fall in love

Help with Writing

Try to make your readers interested in your story. One way to do this is to give them a question they want to find the answer to. For example, the opening sentence of *The Strange Tale of Jim Garry's Mountain* is 'It was the Mayor who saw it first'. The writer doesn't tell us what 'it' is, so we want to read to find out.

2 **You are going to write a short story about something strange that happens in a village. You must write it in the simple past. Before you write your story, plan it, by making notes about the following:**

- The type of story (e.g. science-fiction, fantasy)
- The characters
- The plot

3 **Now write your short story. Use *The Strange Tale of Jim Garry's Mountain* and your notes from Exercise 2 to help you.**

③ Past continuous

> It was 3 o'clock in the afternoon. Burak **was climbing** a tree. Our ball was stuck in one of the branches. Burak got the ball, but he fell and broke his arm.

Super Grammar

Use the **past continuous** to talk about events that were happening at a particular moment in the past, e.g. *Onur was climbing a mountain.*

Form the past continuous with *was/were* + verb + *ing*:

I/he/she was watching a TV about firefighters.
We/you/they were playing football in the garden.

1 Circle the correct verbs to complete the text.

On Saturday afternoon, everyone ¹ _was_ / were doing something.
My brother Pablo ² *was* / *were* reading about the Great Fire of London.
My parents ³ *was* / *were* cleaning the kitchen. My sister Lucia ⁴ *was* / *were* playing a computer game called 'Emergency!' My cousins Maria and Gonzalo ⁵ *was* / *were* painting. I ⁶ *was* / *were* doing something too. Can you guess what it was? Yes, that's right! I ⁷ *was* / *were* watching what everyone else was doing!

2 Match the 1–6 with a–f.

1 I was

2 My brother was

3 My grandparents were

4 My sisters were in

5 My dog was

6 Sarah, my best friend, was

a chasing the cat round the garden. That's her favourite thing to do.

b at home watching a TV programme about the emergency services. Grandma said it was very interesting.

c making a web page on the internet. She's very good with technology.

d the kitchen, making their favourite type of pizza – bananas and onion. Urghhhhh!

e sleeping. He's always tired. He works really hard in school.

f doing my Science homework. I didn't enjoy doing it because it was really hard!

3 Correct the verbs in sentences 1–5. Make past continuous sentences.

1 The firefighters were climb the ladder.
   The firefighters were climbing the ladder.

2 The police officers were ran very quickly.
   _____

3 Sara was make a sandwich.
   _____

4 The paramedic were working very hard.
   _____

5 My friends was watching a film about a flood.
   _____

4 Complete the sentences so they are true for you.

1 On Saturday morning I _____

2 On Saturday afternoon my parents _____

3 On Saturday evening my family _____

4 On Sunday morning I _____

5 On Sunday afternoon my friends and I _____

6 On Sunday evening I _____

Past continuous questions

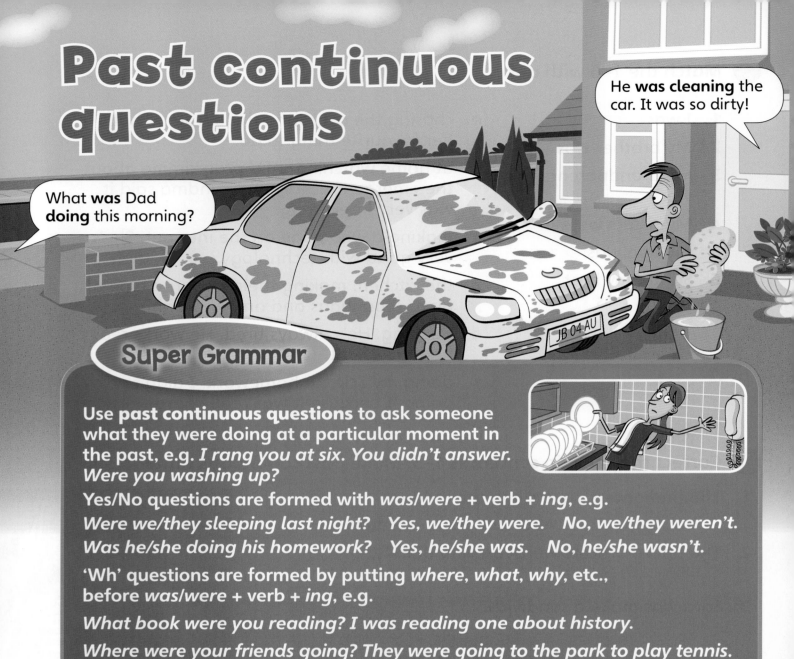

What **was** Dad **doing** this morning?

He **was cleaning** the car. It was so dirty!

Super Grammar

Use **past continuous questions** to ask someone what they were doing at a particular moment in the past, e.g. *I rang you at six. You didn't answer. Were you washing up?*

Yes/No questions are formed with *was/were* + verb + *ing*, e.g.

Were we/they sleeping last night?   Yes, we/they were.   No, we/they weren't.

Was he/she doing his homework?   Yes, he/she was.   No, he/she wasn't.

'Wh' questions are formed by putting *where, what, why,* etc., before *was/were* + verb + *ing*, e.g.

What book were you reading? I was reading one about history.

Where were your friends going? They were going to the park to play tennis.

1 Make questions from the prompts.

1 you / were / what / yesterday / doing / ?   <u>What were you doing yesterday?</u>

2 you / were / sleeping / ?

3 what / friend / doing / was / your / ?

4 was / book / she / reading / a / ?

5 going / you / were / where / ?

6 at / brother / three / doing / your / was / what / o'clock / ?

2 Complete the questions with *was/were* and the verbs from the box in the correct form. Then write the answers.

play   drink   read   run   sit   clean   ~~eat~~

1 ___Was___ the man in the blue T-shirt _cleaning_ the window? _Yes, he was_ .

2 _____ the man in a red T-shirt _____ a pizza? Yes, he _____ .

3 _____ the two women _____ water? No, they _____ .

4 _____ the woman in the red dress _____ down? Yes, she _____ .

5 _____ the police officer _____ after a man? Yes, he _____ .

6 _____ the man with glasses _____ a book? No, he _____ .

3 Complete the questions. Then write true answers for you.

1 What / you / do / four o'clock / afternoon / Monday?
    What were you doing at four o'clock in the afternoon on Monday?

2 What / you / do / six o'clock / morning / Wednesday?

_____

3 What / you / do / 5 o'clock / afternoon / Friday?

_____

4 What / you / do / 9 o'clock / evening / Saturday?

_____

5 What / you / do / 6 o'clock / morning / Sunday?

_____

Reading: an email

1 Read the email, then answer the questions.

To grannyandgranpa@oldpeopleemail.com
Subject The Great Flood Of Calle Dos Santos

Hi Granny,

I've got some news – we had an accident today. Don't worry, everyone is all right. Mum is going to call you later.

It happened yesterday afternoon. We were in Calle Dos Santos, on our way to the cinema. Suddenly, we noticed that there was water ahead of us on the road. It was coming into the car! It all happened so quickly. One minute we were driving along, and then … 'Everyone out!' said Dad. We got out, but Dad caught his leg on the door. We called the emergency services. The police were the first to arrive. The firefighters came next because there were lots of cars that were stuck. They had to pull them out. Then the paramedics came. 'You must keep your leg still,' said one of them to Dad. His leg was really hurting him, but it wasn't broken. The paramedics gave us special emergency blankets to keep warm. I really liked wearing mine and asked if I could take it home.

I've got to go now, Granny. Dad can't walk very well at the moment, so he wants me to go to the kitchen and make him a cup of tea!

Email soon with all your news!

Love,

Valentina

---

1 When did the accident happen? _It happened yesterday afternoon_ .
2 Where were Valentina and her parents going? _____
3 What happened? _____
4 What did Valentina's Dad hurt? _____
5 Who arrived after the police officers? _____
6 What did they give Valentina's family? _____

Writing

1 **Write the phrases from the box in the correct part of the table.**

Bye for now   Hi _____   Dear _____   Email me soon   Best wishes
How are you?   Hello _____   Is everything OK?   How are things?

Starting an email	
Asking how someone is	
Finishing an email	

Help with Writing

When you tell someone your news in an email, give them
the important information, but do not write too much.

2 **You are going to write an email to Valentina telling her all about a fire in a local cafe. Before you write, make notes about the following:**

- When and where the fire started
- What you were doing when it started
- What the firefighters said and did

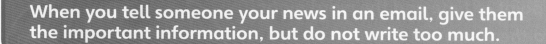

To   valentina@hispanomail.com
Subject   The fire in the cafe

Hello Valentina,
Thanks for your email! _____

_____

_____

_____

Send me another email soon!
Love,

When does the next train to Bilbao leave?

It goes **at** half past 12.

Super Grammar

At/in/on are prepositions. Use them to talk about days, dates, times of the day, periods of time or when things take place, e.g. *I was born at 9 o'clock in the morning in December.*
Use *at* with a point of time and the word *night*.

We're going to the cinema at 6 o'clock.
My brother can't sleep at night.

Use *in* with months of the year, the seasons, years, and the phrases *the morning* and *the afternoon*.

My sister's birthday is in summer, in July.
I was born in 2004.
What did you do in the afternoon?

Use *on* with days of the week and with *morning, afternoon, evening* and *night* when you put the day before those words.

We've got a History test on Wednesday.
What time does the bus leave on Saturday morning?

1. **Complete the sentences with *in, on* or *at*.**

1   Is your birthday __in__ June?
2   That film you want to see starts _____ six o'clock.
3   We're all going to the beach _____ Saturday.
4   We went to my cousins' house _____ Sunday afternoon.
5   What time do you go to bed _____ night?
6   The train leaves at four o'clock _____ the afternoon.

2 Correct the sentences.

1 My birthday is on October.
   My birthday is in October .

2 The film starts in 7 o'clock.
   _____

3 We went swimming in the sea on the morning.
   _____

4 My uncle and aunt came to our house for dinner at Sunday.
   _____

5 Did you see Sean at Tuesday?
   _____

6 We're going to park in Saturday afternoon.
   _____

3 Match 1–6 with a–f.

1	Did you sister move to Barcelona in	a	in summer. Our favourite spot is next to the river.
2	The dog next door to us always barks	b	on Saturday. It's going to be hot!
3	What did you do	c	2012 or 2013?
4	I'd like to go to the beach	d	at 4:00 or does it go at 4:15?
5	Is your birthday in	e	the afternoon when I come home from school.
6	Does the bus leave	f	November or December? Mine is in January.
7	I usually go to bed	g	at 9:30 in the week. I need lots of sleep!
8	My friends and I love to have picnics	h	at exactly 12 o'clock!
9	My grandparents always have lunch	i	in the morning? Did you go swimming?
10	I do my homework in	j	at night. Sometimes, I can't sleep. It's very noisy!

Past continuous and simple past

We **were playing tennis** when it **started** to rain.

Super Grammar

Use **past continuous** and **simple past** together to talk about one action interrupting another in the past.

When you describe two actions using these tenses, you can order the sentence in two ways. You can put the past continuous action first followed by the **simple past**:

I was doing my homework when my computer broke.

You can also put the **simple past** first followed by the past continuous. When you write the sentence in this way, use a comma.

When my computer broke, I was doing my homework.

1 Complete the sentences with the correct form of the verbs from the box Use either the past continuous or simple past.

meet   play   ~~wait~~   do   fall   wait

1 I _was waiting_ for the train when I saw my friend.
2 When my brother came home I _____ my homework.
3 We were playing football when it _____ to snow.
4 Mum was living in Ankara when she _____ Dad.
5 My brother _____ basketball when he broke his leg.
6 My sister doing my Geography homework when she _____ asleep.

2 Circle the correct words to complete the sentences.

1 When I (bumped) / *was bumping* into the tree, I was running after the football.

2 I *watched* / *was watching* TV when you called me.

3 When we *were seeing* / *saw* Miss Gunn the History teacher, we were waiting for a train.

4 We *were sunbathing* / *sunbathed* when it started to rain. We ran into a café nearby to stay dry!

5 My Dad was walking down the street when he *was finding* / *found* the bag.

6 My brother was making a salad for lunch when he *cut* / *was cutting* his finger.

3 Write the underlined verbs in the story in the simple past or past continuous.

I ¹<u>am walking</u> through the park on my way home from town when I ²<u>see</u> a large bear standing in front of me. It ³<u>is playing</u> the violin. 'Good afternoon,' ⁴<u>says</u> the bear.' 'Oh,' I ⁵<u>say</u>, 'good afternoon.' I ⁶<u>am thinking</u> of starting to run, when the bear ⁷<u>says</u> 'I'm not a real bear, you know. This is just a special suit. I'm playing at a children's party later.' The bear ⁸<u>wants</u> to do a bit of practise before the show. I ⁹<u>listen</u> for a while. She ¹⁰<u>isn't</u> bad, for a bear.

1   was walking
2
3
4
5

6
7
8
9
10

Reading: a newspaper article

1 Read the newspaper article, then answer the questions.

The Globe

5th March 2016

DOG ROLLS DOWN ESCALATOR

There was great excitement at King's Cross this morning when a small dog rolled all the way down an escalator. Cuddles, a three-year-old Yorkshire Terrier belonging to Mrs Cynthia Bolton, 48, of Newcastle, wasn't hurt, but his owner was shocked.

Mrs Bolton said. 'We bought our tickets at the ticket office and then walked to the escalator. Cuddles and I were standing at the top of it, when I heard

the announcer make his announcement: 'The train now arriving at Platform 4 is the 9:52 to Glasgow.' 'Quick!' I said to Cuddles. 'That's our train!' I ran forward, slipped on a bit of paper on the floor and dropped the dog. Cuddles rolled all the way down the escalator, landing in a rucksack at the bottom. Before I knew what was happening, I saw a man pick up the rucksack – with Cuddles inside – and walk on to the train. 'Stop!' I shouted. 'That man's got my Cuddles!' '

Other passengers were also surprised. 'We were walking up the stairs,' said John Maloney.

'What happened was just amazing! We put our suitcases down and stopped where we were. We wanted to see what was going on.'

Mrs Bolton didn't think twice. She ran down the escalator as fast she could, jumped on to the train, found the passenger and managed to get her dog back. Cuddles was fine and the pair made their journey home.

1   How old is Mrs Bolton? __48__ .
2   What platform did the announcer talk about? _____
3   What was Mrs Bolton doing when she heard the announcement?

_____
4   What did Mrs Bolton slip on? _____
5   What did Cuddles fall into? _____

Writing

1 **Complete the table with the information from the box.**

> 'It was terrible. They walked on without paying for a ticket.'
> 'Everyone must pay to use the service. The rules are for everyone.'
> Two boys got on to a train without a ticket
> The transport police asked the boys to get off the train
> On platform 3 at Liverpool Street Station in London

What happened	
Where it happened	
What people said	
What happened in the end	

Help with Writing

Newspaper articles often include things that people said about the story. Reporters do this to make their articles more interesting for the reader.

2 **Imagine you write for a newspaper. Write an article about what happened at Liverpool Street Station. Use the information in Exercise 1 and the newspaper article about Cuddles to help you. Include:**

- A title for the article
- The names of the two boys.
- Where they wanted to go.
- The names of the people in Exercise 1.

5 Used to

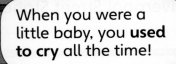

When you were a little baby, you **used to cry** all the time!

Super Grammar

Use **used to** to talk about things you did routinely in the past, or the way things were in the past.
e.g. *My grandmother used to be a teacher.*
She used to teach Spanish.

When we use *used to* we are saying that things are different now:

My sister used to play the piano. (She doesn't play it now.)
My brother used to draw cartoons. (He doesn't draw them now.)

1 **Complete the sentences with the verbs from the box.**

be ~~have~~ live play work make

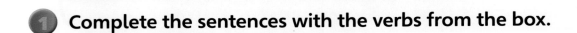

The other day I was thinking about how things change. For example, I used to ¹ *have* blonde hair when I was younger. It's dark now. My friends and I used to ² _____ football every Saturday morning, but these days we never do that. I used to ³ _____ with my parents and brother in a small flat in the centre of our city, but now we live in a big house with a garden in a village outside the city. Dad used to ⁴ _____ for a newspaper, but now he works for a website. Mum used to ⁵ _____ a children's television programme called Milkshake, but now she writes stories. Grandad used to ⁶ _____ a police officer, but now he is retired. Nothing stays the same. It can *be* sad sometimes, but it keeps things interesting!

2 **Are the sentences correct or incorrect? Correct the sentences you think are wrong.**

1 David use to carry a walkie-talkie.

 Incorrect. _David used to carry a walkie-talkie._

2 Tina used to interview suspects.

_____

3 Brian used to work in a police station.

_____

4 Jerry used to wearing a uniform.

_____

5 Chris using to catch criminals.

_____

6 Jonathan used drive a fast car.

_____

3 **Write sentences with *used to*. Then write what the person does or has now.**

1 Ceren _used to play basketball._
   Now she plays tennis

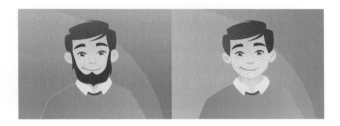

2 Sandro _____

3 Elena _____

4 Sam _____

Had to

I'm so tired! I **had to study** all day for my big English exam tomorrow.

Super Grammar

Use **had to** to talk about something that someone told you do, e.g. *Dad had to paint the fence at the weekend. Mum told him it was looking a bit dirty.*

1 **Rewrite the sentences with the words in the correct order.**

1   rooms / tidy / we/ to / had   We had to tidy our rooms.
2   had / homework / to / his / Dom / do
3   to / wash / dishes / had / the / Marlene / up
4   had / clean / to / the / Sofia / windows
5   Neil / sweep / floor / had / the / to
6   walk / dog / had / Ada / to / the
7   cook / had/ Pablo / to / meal / the / evening
8   early / bed / had / Zehra / to / to / go

2 Circle the correct verbs to complete the text.

My brother went to a Police Academy last year. Things weren't easy there! They had to ¹ (start) / starting at 6:00. They had to ² wore / wear a uniform. They had to ³ go / goes running every day. They had to ⁴ spent / spend two hours every evening doing homework. They had to ⁵ did / do tests about how to be a police officer every Monday morning. Oh, and they had to ⁶ attend / attending on Saturday mornings too! He enjoyed it, but he's happy he doesn't have to go there now.

3 Look at the pictures. Then write sentences using *had to* and the verbs from the box.

> cook dinner   do the shopping   study for an exam   take   wash up   clean the bathroom

1   Mick _had to do the shopping_ for his grandma.

2   Marco _____ for his family.

3   Mia _____ at the weekend.

4   Pedro _____ after dinner.

5   Stephanie _____ before she could watch TV.

6   Katya _____ her little sister to school.

Reading: a description

1 Read the blog post, then complete the sentences.

LOU'S BLOG ABOUT SCHOOL
March 9th, 2016

Describing Detectives!

We had a really interesting class this morning. We talked about detectives. Detectives are a special type of police officer. Their job is to investigate serious crimes like murder. 'My sister used to be a detective,' said Mr Garcia. 'Wow!' I said. 'Did she enjoy the job?' 'Yes, she did,' said Mr Garcia, 'but it wasn't easy.' Then he told us all about his sister's job. She used to work at night and used to work long hours. She had to look for clues. She had to interview suspects. She had to work really hard to solve the murders.

Later, Mr Garcia asked us to describe a detective from the past. But he didn't want us to describe a real detective, we had to invent one. We had to give our detective a name and describe his or her daily life. I called my detective Inspector Bach. This was my description of him: Inspector Bach didn't have any hair, but he had a beard and moustache. There was a scar on the end of his nose. He liked to touch the scar. Inspector Bach used to work on solving murders. He used to solve his crimes in an unusual way – by listening to music. 'I always get my best ideas then,' he said. Inspector Bach used to work on his own. 'I like to be quiet,' he said, 'it helps me think.'

😊 😐 😞
(10 comments)

1   Mr Garcia's sister used to be a ___detective.___ .
2   Mr Garcia's sister _____ for clues.
3   Mr Garcia asked Lou's class to invent their own _____.
4   Lou called his detective _____.
5   Lou's detective _____ his crimes by listening to music.

Writing

1 Describe members of your family. Use the words from the box.

> beard   moustache   blonde   fair   dark   curly   straight   long   short

1 _____

2 _____

3 _____

4 _____

5 _____

Help with Writing

When you write a description of someone, you want the reader to 'see' the person. You can do this by using interesting details. For example, Lou tells us that Inspector Bach had a scar on the end of his nose.

2 Invent a detective from the past. Write a description of him or her. Use Lou's description of Inspector Bach to help you. Include:

● Your detective's name.

● A description of his or her hair, eyes, height, etc.

● The things your detective used to do and had to do.

My detective: January 6th, 2016

_____

_____

_____

_____

_____

Comparatives and superlatives

The Tyrannosaurus Rex is one of the most **well-known** of the dinosaurs, but it was not the biggest. The Titanosaurs were much **bigger**.

Tyrannosaurus Rex

Super Grammar

Use **comparatives** to compare two people, places or things, e.g. *Josep is faster than Marco.*

There are some rules to learn:

Add -*er* to the end of adjectives with one syllable, e.g. slower

Put *more* before adjectives of two or more syllables, e.g. more difficult

There are some irregular forms, e.g. better, worse

Use **superlatives** to say one thing or person in a group has the most of a particular quality, e.g. *Josep is the fastest runner I know.*

Add -*est* to the end of adjectives with one syllable, e.g. slowest

Put *the most* before adjectives of two or more syllables, e.g. *the most difficult*

There are some irregular forms, e.g. *the best, the worst*

1 Write the comparatives and the superlatives.

1 big   *bigger*   *the biggest*

2 strong

3 heavy

4 friendly

5 dangerous

6 beautiful

2 Rewrite the sentences with the words in the correct order.

1 lions / are / smaller / domestic / than / much / cats / .
   Domestic cats are much smaller than lions.

2 in / biggest / world / some / the / are / animals / elephants / the / of / .

_____

3 interesting / beasts / are / than / real / more / mythical / animals / .

_____

4 are / dangerous/ the / Africa / mosquitos / animals / in / most / ?

_____

5 fastest / cheetah / animal / the / the / land / is / .

_____

6 necks / kangaroos / than / giraffes / longer / have / .

_____

3 Complete the text with the comparative or superlative form of the adjectives.

My parents gave me a great present for my birthday – *The Dictionary of Mythical Beasts*. It was the **1** most interesting (interesting) book I knew. It taught me about mermaids, Pegasus and the Sphinx. I read it every morning before breakfast and every night before I fell asleep. One evening, after dinner, I couldn't find it anywhere. 'Oh, no!' I said, 'this is **2** _____ (bad) day of my life! Where is my book, Fred? Help me!' But my brother was too busy playing *The Phoenix Rises*, his new video game. 'This is much **3** _____ (exciting) than your old book,' he said. 'No, it's not,' I said. 'My book teaches me things. Your game is just for fun.' 'But when I play this,' said Fred, 'I learn how to see things that move quickly. I *see* **4** them _____ (good) than I did before. This morning, for example, I saw Roger running really fast into the garden.' Roger was our dog. 'He had something in his mouth. It looked **5** _____ (heavy) than his toy bones. I took it from him *before* he could chew it. Have a look over there.' I found my book in Roger's basket. On its cover were marks from Roger's teeth, but it was OK. 'Thanks Fred,' I said. 'You're **6** _____ (good) brother in the world! Can you show me how to play *The Phoenix Rises*?'

It looks like ...

It looks like a really big ape!

Super Grammar

Use **it looks like** to talk about the appearance of someone or something, e.g. *Unicorns look like horses.*
The phrase is used to ask about someone or something's appearance.

What does your brother look like? He's tall and has got short black hair.

Note that we do not use looks like in the reply.

It's also used to compare appearances.

Who does your sister look like? She looks like my Mum.
Look at the cloud! It looks like a face.

1 **Correct the sentences.**

1 Who are your brother look like?

   Who does your brother look like?

2 Who do you looking like?

3 Does a centaur looks like a man?

4 What do mermaids look liking?

2 Match the answers with the question in Exercise 1.

a Well, I've got short black hair and brown eyes. I look like my Dad. _____

b He looks a little bit like my Mum. They've both got long noses. __1__

c Yes and no. They've got the head and body of a man, but the legs of a horse. _____

d They look like women, but with fish tails instead of legs. _____

3 Complete the description with the words from the box.

like   it   looks   does   ~~look~~

The Dictionary of MYTHICAL BEASTS

L is for the Loch Ness Monster

What do mythical creatures ¹ look like? Well, they are all different. It depends on the imagination of their creators. The Loch Ness Monster is the most famous mythical beast of the United Kingdom. People come from all over the world, hoping to see this creature swimming about in a large lake in the highlands of Scotland.

What ² _____ it look like? Nobody knows, of course, but some people who believe it exists say that it ³ _____ like a dinosaur, other says ⁴ _____ looks like a dragon. It's got a long neck and a small head. Have a look at the picture. What do you think it looks ⁵ _____?

Reading: a description of an animal

1 Read about the babirusa, then complete descriptions a–e with words from the box.

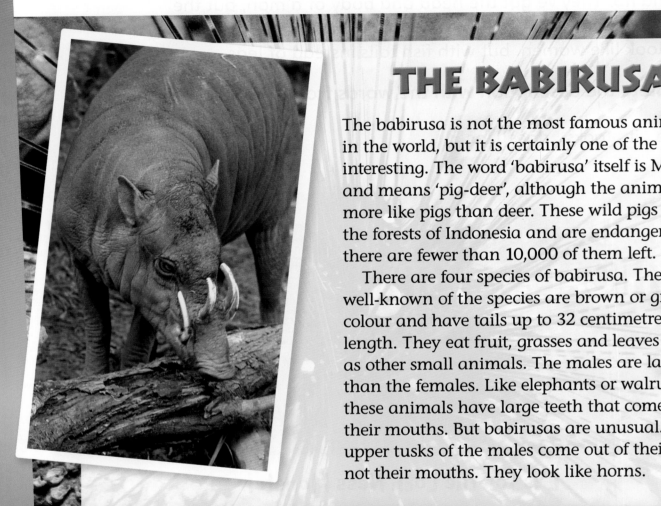

THE BABIRUSA

The babirusa is not the most famous animal in the world, but it is certainly one of the most interesting. The word 'babirusa' itself is Malay and means 'pig-deer', although the animals look more like pigs than deer. These wild pigs live in the forests of Indonesia and are endangered – there are fewer than 10,000 of them left.

There are four species of babirusa. The most well-known of the species are brown or grey in colour and have tails up to 32 centimetres in length. They eat fruit, grasses and leaves as well as other small animals. The males are larger than the females. Like elephants or walruses, these animals have large teeth that come out of their mouths. But babirusas are unusual. The upper tusks of the males come out of their snouts not their mouths. They look like horns.

deer t̶u̶s̶k̶s̶ walrus forest snout

a A pair of large pointed teeth, like those of an elephant. _tusks_

b An animal that moves fast. The males have horns called 'antlers'. _____

c A large area of land covered with trees. _____

d The nose of an animal, especially that of a pig. _____

e An animal that lives in and around the sea in the North Pole. It has thick fur and two long tusks. _____

Writing

1 Complete the table with the information from the box.

the rainforests of Madagascar   Aye-aye
Have got big eyes and ears, and have a tail larger than their body
Don't look like primates, but are related to apes, chimps and humans
Are nocturnal, so sleep in the day   insects and fruit
Spend their lives in trees

Name	
Where it lives	
What it looks like	
How it lives	
What it eats	

2 Write about the Aye-Aye. Use the information in the table in Exercise 1 and the description of the babirusa to help you.

Help with Writing

A short description of animal should give as much information as possible in a few words. Try to answer possible questions in your description. e.g. *How big is it? How long does it live?*

7 Possessive pronouns

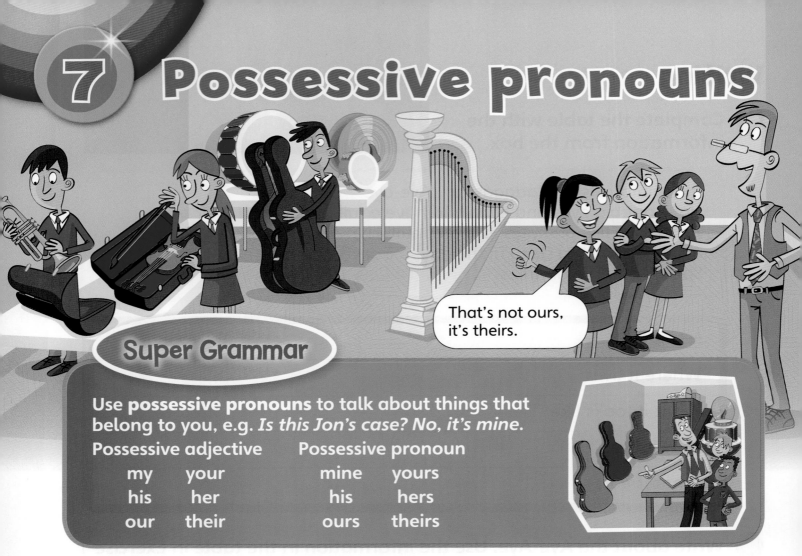

That's not ours, it's theirs.

Super Grammar

Use **possessive pronouns** to talk about things that belong to you, e.g. *Is this Jon's case? No, it's mine.*

Possessive adjective		Possessive pronoun	
my	your	mine	yours
his	her	his	hers
our	their	ours	theirs

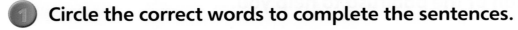

1 Circle the correct words to complete the sentences.

1 Is this Leo's coat?

Yes, it's *hers* / *his*.

2 Look! These are *his* / *our* scooters!

Yes! That's Raul's and that's yours, Antonio!

3 Is that her violin?

No, it's not. *Hers* / *Mine* is over there.

4 These aren't my pencils? Are they *yours* / *hers*?

No, they're not mine.

5 Are you sure this violin is Tom and Deb's?

Yes, it's *theirs* / *ours*. I saw them with it earlier.

6 Is that the guitar you parents got you for your birthday?

No, it isn't. Mine/yours is at home.

2 **Rewrite the sentences with possessive pronouns.**

1 It's my tractor. ___It's mine.___

2 Is that your car? _____

3 That's his book. _____

4 It's her keyboard. _____

5 These are our instruments. _____

6 Are these their bags? _____

3 **Replace the underlined words with possessive pronouns.**

It was my saxophone, not Toni's. 'This is [1]my saxophone,' Toni said. 'It's not [2]her saxophone,' I said to my friend. 'It's [3]my saxophone.' Toni had her own saxophone. 'That's [4]your saxophone,' I said. 'But I don't like that one,' she said, This happened all the time. Toni always wanted what other people had. 'Harry brought his keyboard to school today,' she told me once. 'He wanted to practise at lunchtime. I told him it wasn't [5]his keyboard.' 'Whose did you say it was?' I asked, knowing what the answer was going to be. '[6]My keyboard!'

One morning, at breakfast, I decided to let Toni know what she was like. She sat down at the table with some toast. 'Thanks for the toast,' I said. 'It's not [7]your toast,' she said. 'No, it's not' I said. 'It's [8]my toast.' I did this every day for a week. She wasn't very happy with me, but I didn't stop saying that all the toast she made was [9]my toast. 'OK, OK,' she said, a week later. 'It's [10]your toast and my toast.'

1 _____mine_____   6 _____

2 _____   7 _____

3 _____   8 _____

4 _____   9 _____

5 _____   10 _____

Who/which/where

This is the house where Callum lives.

Super Grammar

Who/which/where are relative pronouns. Use these words to give more information about a person, thing or place.

*Anya's the girl **who** lives in my street.*
*The book **which** I got for my birthday is called How To Play The Drums.*
*The town **where** Omer lives has got a great new cinema.*

1 Circle the correct relative pronouns to complete the sentences.

1 The theatre _____ we played our first concert is the oldest in our town.

    a who   **b** which   **c** (where)

2 The biscuits _____ my brother and sister made are delicious.

    a who   **b** which   **c** where

3 The girl _____ joined our class last week is from Bodrum.

    a who   **b** which   **c** where

4 The video game _____ I bought at the weekend is brilliant.

    a who   **b** which   **c** where

5 The town _____ my grandparents live is high in the mountains.

    a who   **b** which   **c** where

6 The boy _____ lives next door to us plays the harp really well.

    a who   **b** which   **c** where

2 **Tick the correct sentences.**

1 **a** Yesterday I bought a keyboard which is from the US. ✓
  b Yesterday I bought a keyboard who is from the US. _____

2 **a** Look, there's the girl where lives next door to my grandparents! _____
  b Look, there's the girl who lives next door to my grandparents! _____

3 **a** The car which my brother drives is black. _____
  b The car who my brother drives is black. _____

4 **a** Martina is the girl who comes from the north of Spain. _____
  b Martina is the girl where comes from the north of Spain. _____

5 **a** The park which we play tennis is near my house. _____
  b The park where we play tennis is near my house. _____

6 **a** The instrument who Furkan plays is the piano. _____
  b The instrument which Furkan plays is the piano. _____

3 **Complete the information about the festival with *who*, *which* or *where*.**

Summer Fest

Summer Fest is for people ¹ _who_ love all types of music. It's the festival ² _____ everyone enjoys!

We've got jazz, pop, rock, classical and hip hop. Oh, and folk too! And we've got the perfect location. Hendrix Hall is the place ³ _____ the festival happens. It's got a lake, tree-lined walks and lots of picnic spots.

Tickets cost £60. For people ⁴ _____ are under 16 we've even got a special price – £45!

Mat and Jen are the people ⁵ _____ organise the festival. They know everything! If you want to ask them a question, email them at mattandjen@summermusic.com. But the only thing ⁶ _____ you really need to know is this: be ready to dance! See you there.

Reading: an advertisement

1 Read the advertisement, then complete the sentences.

The perfect guitar for rock and roll!

Des Paul designed **The Fretocaster** in 1956.

It's the instrument of the guitar heroes who made musical history.

Today, well-known Guitarists such as Peter Brown, Derick Cloptan and Johnny Book play this beautiful instrument.

And now it can be yours for a VERY SPECIAL PRICE!

For <u>one week only</u> you can buy your very own Des Paul for **£350**! That's is 50% cheaper than normal! What are you waiting for? Buy a Des Paul Fretocaster now!

Available in all good music shops or at <u>www.despaul.com</u>.

1 Des Paul created the guitar in _____1956_____ .
2 Many famous _____ play the Des Paul.
3 It usually costs _____ .
4 You can buy it for a special price – _____ .
5 The special price is available for only _____ .
6 You can buy the guitar online or in _____ .

Writing

1 **Add more instruments to the instrument word families below.**

String family	*guitar*
Percussion family	
Brass family	

Help with Writing

Adverts try to make readers feel something. When we are excited or happy advertisers think we are more likely to want to spend money. Look at the advert for the guitar. The Des Paul is 'beautiful' and it's 'the instrument of guitar heroes'. The advert uses these phrases to make people want to own one of the guitars for themselves.

2 **Write an advertisement for a musical instrument. Use the advertisement for the Fretocaster to help you write yours. Include:**

- the name of the instrument
- people who play it
- places where you can buy it
- types of music which you can play with it
- price

8 Will

What will you be when you grow up?

I'll **be** an astronaut and visit Mars!

Super Grammar

Use **will** to make predictions about the future, e.g. I think *Patrick will be a football* player.

Yes/No question form

Will we live on the moon one day?
Yes, we will. /No, we won't.

'Wh' question form

What will the weather be like next week?   I think it will be hot and sunny.

The contracted form of *will* is *'ll*, e.g. *I'll, she'll, we'll.*

Difference between *will* and *going to*

Both *will* and *going to* can be used to make predictions. We usually use *going to* when we are more certain that something is going to happen. For example, looking up at a black cloud in the sky, we say 'it's going to rain' not 'it will rain'.

1 **Complete the sentences with the verbs from the box.**

> have   travel   be   live   ~~catch~~   work

1 Will you __catch__ dangerous criminals when you're a police officer, Jess?
2 When I grow up I'll _____ in a hospital.
3 Will we all _____ on the moon one day?
4 I think it will _____ hot at the weekend.
5 When I grow up, my friends and I will _____ around the world.
6 We'll _____ lots of fun at Eliot's birthday party.

2 **Rewrite the sentences with the words in the correct order.**

1 be / what / you / will   _What will you be?_

2 you / will / where / work   _____?

3 will / live / another country / in / you   _____?

4 you / of house / will / what type / in / live   _____?

5 meet / you / who / will   _____?

6 where / will / travel / you   _____?

7 learn / will / you / what / languages   _____?

8 will / you / what / do / your / free time / in   _____?

3 **Answer the questions in Exercise 2 so they are true for you.**

My Future Blog

My Future

I was thinking about my future the other day. These are my predictions for my life …

1 _____

2 _____

3 _____

4 _____

5 _____

6 _____

7 _____

8 _____

Adverbs

It was the last day of school before the summer holidays. The children walked home, singing songs loudly in the afternoon sun.

Super Grammar

Use **adverbs** to say how someone does, did or will do an action, e.g. *The ambulance driver drove quickly.*

We form many adverbs by adding *-ly* to an adjective:

quick – quickly   bad – badly   loud – loudly

If an adjective ends in *y*, we change the *y* to an *i* and add *-ly*:

angry – angrily   happy – happily   heavy – heavily

Some adverbs have an irregular form:

good – well   hard – hard   fast – fast

1 **Write the adverbs.**

1   quick   *quickly*   4   careful   _____
2   dangerous   _____   5   bad   _____
3   beautiful   _____   6   heavy   _____

2 **Complete the email with the adverb form of the words from the box.**

good
~~quiet~~
loud
happy
slow
quick

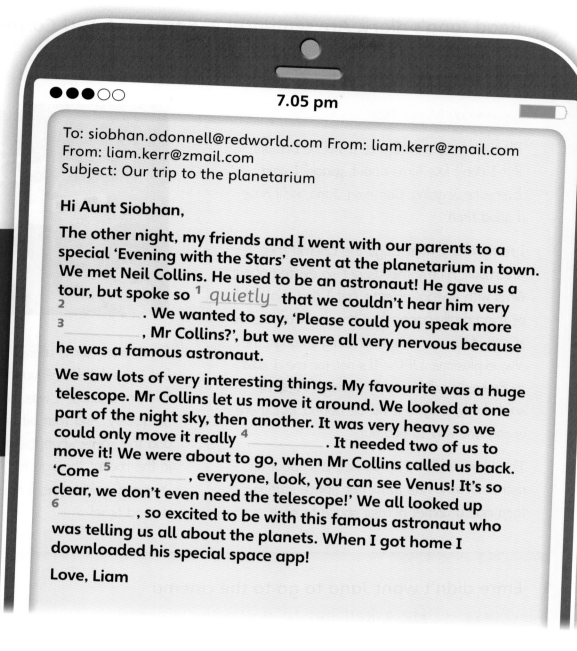

●●●○○   7.05 pm

To: siobhan.odonnell@redworld.com From: liam.kerr@zmail.com
From: liam.kerr@zmail.com
Subject: Our trip to the planetarium

Hi Aunt Siobhan,

The other night, my friends and I went with our parents to a special 'Evening with the Stars' event at the planetarium in town. We met Neil Collins. He used to be an astronaut! He gave us a tour, but spoke so ¹ _quietly_ that we couldn't hear him very ² _____ . We wanted to say, 'Please could you speak more ³ _____ , Mr Collins?', but we were all very nervous because he was a famous astronaut.

We saw lots of very interesting things. My favourite was a huge telescope. Mr Collins let us move it around. We looked at one part of the night sky, then another. It was very heavy so we could only move it really ⁴ _____ . It needed two of us to move it! We were about to go, when Mr Collins called us back. 'Come ⁵ _____ , everyone, look, you can see Venus! It's so clear, we don't even need the telescope!' We all looked up ⁶ _____ , so excited to be with this famous astronaut who was telling us all about the planets. When I got home I downloaded his special space app!

Love, Liam

3 **Complete the sentences with adverbs.**

1   My granddad drove so _slowly_ so that it took us a long time to get home.
2   My brother ran _____ and won the race.
3   I walked _____ downstairs because I didn't want anyone to hear me.
4   Hold that _____ , Tom! You don't want to drop it.
5   My sister did _____ on her English exam. She got 89%!
6   I played _____ and lost the tennis match 6–2, 6–1.

Reading: a diary entry

1 **Read Jana's diary. Are sentences 1–5 true or false? Correct the false sentences.**

Wednesday March 16th

'Please come,' said Emre, 'it will be brilliant!' 'But I don't like films about space,' I said. 'Everyone is going. Come on, Jana, we'll have a good time.'

I really didn't want to go the cinema this afternoon. All my friends get so excited about films with special effects, but I find that sort of thing really boring. You know, astronauts on space stations, rockets whizzing through the sky, explosions, UFOs. It's not for me. I said to Emre: 'It will be really boring.' 'Well,' he said slowly, 'maybe it will be boring, but there is only one way to find out.'

The film is called The Comet. It's about an astronaut who has to fix her space station, then ride a comet across space to save

Earth from some aliens. Really, really silly. But I loved it! Emre laughed at me after the film because I was talking so much and so quickly. 'And that bit with the two moons, and the scene when the astronaut went up in the rocket through the stars, and, and ...!' 'You see,' said Emre, 'I knew you would have a good time!'

1 Emre didn't want Jana to go to the cinema

  False.   _He asked her to go to the cinema._

2 Jana didn't want to go to the cinema.

_____

3 Jana likes films about space.

_____

4 Jana thought the idea for the film was very interesting.

_____

5 Jana liked the film.

_____

Writing

1 **Complete the phrases from the diary with the words from the box.**

everyone   brilliant   be   'll   ~~come~~

1 Please ____come.____ .
2 It will be _____ .
3 _____ is going.
4 We _____ have a good time.
5 It will _____ really boring.

Help with Writing

People often write diaries to record not only their feelings, but also the most interesting things that they do. This means that in the future, they can look back at the past and remember some of their favourite times.

2 **Write a diary entry for one day last week. Try to use *will* and adverbs. Choose one of the following two events to write an entry about:**

- You went to the cinema with your friends. You watched a film about an astronaut. You wanted to go, but didn't like the film.
- You went to the planetarium with your family. You learn about the planets. You didn't want to go, but you had a good time.

_____
_____
_____
_____
_____
_____
_____
_____

⑨ A bottle/can/loaf/ packet/piece of ...

OK, for our picnic, we need two loaves of bread, a bottle of water and a big piece of cheese!

Super Grammar

Use **a bottle / can / loaf / packet / piece of** to talk about the quantity of something or what something is contained in.
Use *bottle* with water, orange juice, lemonade, milk.
Use *can* with lemonade, tomatoes, pears, carrots.
Use *loaf* with bread. The plural is *loaves*.
Use *packet* with biscuits, crisps.
Use *piece of* with cheese, cake.

1 **Correct the sentences.**

1 Can we take a loaf of biscuits, please?

 Can we take a packet of biscuits, please?

2 I'm going to buy a bottle of tomatoes from the shop.

_____

3 Who would like this last can of cake?

_____

4 We need a bottle of crisps and some chocolate.

_____

5 I'd like two cans of bread, please.

_____

6 There was a new piece of milk in the fridge yesterday.

_____

2 **Complete the dialogue with the words from the box.**

> piece   bottles   packets   bottle   ~~loaf~~   pieces   packet   loaves

Marie: We've got one ¹__loaf__ of bread? Is that enough?

Carl: No, we need two ²_____ for the four of us.

Marie: OK. What about something to drink?

Carl: Well, Stefan's got two ³_____ of water and I've got a ⁴_____ of orange juice.

Marie: Do we need anything else. A ⁵_____ of biscuits maybe?

Carl: No, Jeremy's got that. You know his sweet tooth. He's going to bring two ⁶_____ of biscuits and a big ⁷_____ of cake for everyone.

Marie: Really? I think that's everything, then? Oh, cheese?

Carl: Got that. I cut three big ⁸_____ this morning and put them in my bag.

Marie: Great!

3 **Use the notes below, and words for containers, to write a shopping list.**

2 x ~~bread~~   1 x biscuit   6 x crisps
3 x milk   2 x tomatoes   1 x carrots
2 x water   1 x pears

Shopping List

1   Two loaves of bread
2   _____
3   _____
4   _____
5   _____
6   _____
7   _____
8   _____

How much?/How many?

How much milk is there, Oscar?

Super Grammar

Use **How much …?** / **How many …?** to ask about the quantity of something, e.g. *How much cheese do we need*?

Use *how much* with uncountable nouns such as cheese, milk, water, rice.

Use *how many* with countable nouns such as carrots, loaves, packets, pieces.

Note that when we use *how many* with an uncountable noun we only make the container plural, e.g. we say, *How many bottles of water?* not, *How many bottles of waters?*

1 Circle the correct words to complete the sentences.

1 How *many* / *much* eggs do you need for the omelette?
2 How *many* / *much* bars of chocolate are there in the cupboard?
3 How *many* / *much* pieces of cheese would you like?
4 How *many* / *much* bottles of milk are there in the fridge?
5 How *many* / *much* bread do you want?
6 How *many* / *much* water do you think we need?

2 **Match the questions in Exercise 1 with the answers below.**

a I can only see one. Mum finished the other bottle this morning.   <u>4</u>

b Get me two small loaves, please.   <u>   </u>

c One big piece.   <u>   </u>

d I think six will be enough.   <u>   </u>

e Quite a lot. It's going to be a hot day.   <u>   </u>

f There aren't any. I think Dad ate them all!   <u>   </u>

3 **Complete the questions about the picture with *much* or *many*.
Then answer them with *There is / There are*.**

1 How <u>many</u> cans of tomatoes are there? *There are two cans of tomatoes*

2 How <u>   </u> packets of crisps are there? <u>   </u>

3 How <u>   </u> bread is there? <u>   </u>

4 How <u>   </u> chocolate is there? <u>   </u>

5 How <u>   </u> apples are there? <u>   </u>

6 How <u>   </u> cans of carrots are there? <u>   </u>

Reading: A letter

1 **Read the letter, then order the information in sentences a–g.**

Dear students,

As you know, next Friday is the camping trip to the Northern Mountains, three days of walking and cooking outdoors – we're all looking forward to it.

    I am writing to you in order to give you some important information about the trip. We set off from the school car park at six o'clock on Friday morning, so please make sure you are at the gates by at least 5:45. That is a very early start, I know – set your alarms!

    It will take two hours to drive to the Northern Mountains. Please bring some music to listen to on the journey, a book to read, or a game of some type to play with your friends. You should also bring a bottle of water and something to eat, perhaps a sandwich, a piece of fruit and a packet of crisps.

    As soon as we get to the campsite, we will put up our tents. The teachers are ready to help students with this. After that, we plan to spend the afternoon outside. There are ropes to swing on and a lake to dive into and swim. Remember to bring your swimsuits! We are going to organise boat trips throughout the weekend. Students can take turns to sail the small boats.

    All students will have special duties over the weekend. Some will make breakfast, others will collect wood. One group will make a big raft. The teachers will tell you on the first day who is in which group.

    One final thing. The question students usually ask before the trip is, 'How many people will sleep in each tent?' I can answer that question now. The tents are very big and four students will sleep in each one.

    If you would like further information about the trip, do not hesitate to call me in my office between 10 am and 2 pm Monday to Friday.

Yours sincerely,
Elanur Berker.

a how long the trip is	**e** when to call the office	
b where the students are going	**f** things students will do	
c how many students in a tent	**g** when the trip starts	1
d things students need to bring		

Writing

1 **Answer the questions about your country.**

1 Where are the best places to go camping?

2 What can you do in those places?

3 When will the weather be best in those places?

Help with Writing

When we write formal letters we begin them with *Dear* ...
When a writer wants to be very formal, he or she can finish
the letter with *Yours sincerely.*

2 **Imagine you are the principal of a school. You are going to write a letter telling students about a camping trip in your country. Plan the letter by making notes. Include:**

● when it is

● where it is

● how long the trip is

● things students need to bring on the trip

● activities students will do on the trip

3 **Now write your letter. Use the letter about and your notes from Exercise 2 to help you.**

Acknowledgements

The authors and publishers acknowledge the following sources of copyright material and are grateful for the permissions granted. While every effort has been made, it has not always been possible to identify the sources of all the material used, or to trace all copyright holders. If any omissions are brought to our notice, we will be happy to include the appropriate acknowledgements on reprinting and in the next update to the digital edition, as applicable.

Key: Ex = Exercise, L = Left, R = Right.

p. 11 (Ex 3.1): Donald Iain Smith/Blend Images/Getty Images; p. 11 (Ex 3.2): charlybutcher/iStock/Getty Images; p. 11 (Ex 3.3): RMAX/iStock/Getty Images; p. 11 (Ex 3.4): Westend61/Westend61/Getty Images; p. 11 (Ex 3.5): Lorenzo Dominguez/Moment/Getty Images; p. 11 (Ex 3.6): Lee Harris/EyeEm/EyeEm/Getty Images; p. 23: Thinkstock/Stockbyte/Getty Images; p. 26: ChrisCrafter/E+/Getty Images; p. 32 (L): Chris Mellor/Lonely Planet Images/Getty Images; p. 32 (R): MonicaNinker/iStock/Getty Images; p. 38: Oppenheim Bernhard/Stone/Getty Images; p. 44: Alphotographic/iStock/Getty Images; p. 45: Danita Delimont/Gallo Images/Getty Images; p. 56: Nick White/DigitalVision/Getty Images.

The publishers are grateful to the following illustrators:

A Corazon Abierto (Sylvie Poggio Artists), Clive Goodyer, Anna Hancock (Beehive), Marek Jagucki, Chris Lensch, Alan Rowe, David Semple